Shout Ha! to the Sky

ROBERT SULLIVAN is a critically acclaimed and award-winning New Zealand Maori poet who is now based in Honolulu and teaches creative writing at the University of Hawai'i. He has performed at festivals in the US, New Zealand, Italy, India, Germany and Canada. As well as five other books of poetry, he has co-edited Whetu Moana (an anthology of Polynesian poetry), Best New Zealand Poems 2006, and co-edits the online journal Trout.

Also by Robert Sullivan

Jazz Waiata (Auckland University Press)
Pike ake! Poems 1990–92 (AUP)
Maui Legends of the Outcast (Godwit)
Star Waka (AUP)
Captain Cook in the Underworld (AUP)
Weaving Earth and Sky: Myths and Legends of Aotearoa
    (Random House NZ)
Voice Carried My Family (AUP)
Whetu Moana: Contemporary Polynesian Poems in English co-
    edited with Albert Wendt and Reina Whaitiri (AUP)

Shout Ha! to the Sky

ROBERT SULLIVAN

LONDON

PUBLISHED BY SALT PUBLISHING
Fourth Floor, 2 Tavistock Place, Bloomsbury, London WC1H 9RA United Kingdom

© Robert Sullivan, 2010

Salt Publishing 2010

Printed and bound in the United Kingdom by MPG Books Group

Typeset in Swift 9.5 / 13

ISBN 978 1 84471 455 1 paperback

1 3 5 7 9 8 6 4 2

Contents

Acknowledgements

Some of these poems first appeared in the following: *Best New Zealand Poems*, *NZ Listener*, *Landfall*, *Poetry New Zealand*, *JAAM*, *Turbine*, *Salt* (ed. John Kinsella, UK), *Yellow Medicine River: A Journal of Indigenous Literature, Art and Thought*, *Endangered Species* (eds Jenny Bornholdt and Gregory O'Brien), *Growing Up Maori* (ed. Witi Ihimaera), *Towards a Transcultural Future* (eds. Peter Marsden and Geoffrey Davis, Germany), *Litterama`ohi* (eds. Flora Devantine and Ra`i a Mai, Tahiti), *Moving Worlds* (UK), *Hawai'i Review*, *Berkeley Poetry Review* and Whangarei City Library which installed the poem I wrote for its new library building.

Many thanks go to Anne Kennedy. Thanks also to John Kinsella for commissioning this book, Chris Hamilton-Emery, Charlotte Prince and to Salt Publishing.

He karakia whakawhetai ki te Atua hei arataki i te wairua.
This is a prayer of thanks to the Creator who guides the spirit.

1. Histories

1 Maui's Alternate Prayer
(with an image from "Sigh" by Stéphane Mallarmé)

Can the sun be drawn out without
          me beating him? Can a yellow
ray soothe the earth like a cool cloth?
          Can the clouds sit on blue a while
longer? Let them push white over
          the snow-flower mountains draping
my island, flowers to make leis
          up for the eyes of my waka.
Let the sun walk gently, longing
          for a good night. Then he can glide.

2 Love Song for Michael King

The Penguin History of New Zealand cover is a picture
of an inlet, scuffed by tussock, and a fire trailing smoke
like a censer touching the white cloud far above it
at the beginning of the tree-line pushed up close
to the feet of the hills. In the background is a taller
range of hills, and if you know the country
there'll be another taller one over the horizon.

The sand of the inlet is decorated with driftwood,
and in between the tussock pokes out heads of flax
with pods ready to drop. The light could be early morning
or evening, it isn't sharp enough to be fully day.
The sand of the inlet isn't covered by water,
and it snakes sideways to where the smoke begins.
Who lit the fire? There isn't a lot to tell.

Michael King's name is below the picture
on the paperback. The vegetation bends
from right to left and inland, so this place is
on one of the west coasts, given our prevailing
nor-westerly flow, I guess near Greymouth
because it seems so empty, and I've been there,
seen ghost stumps sticking out of the morning

mist long after this illustration is set. The trees
were hollowed out then, a cluster of towers in cloud.

Note:

The cover illustration for King's book is by artist Bob Kerr.

3 The Charge of the Brown Brigade

I am weaving flax fuselage—how clever!
That will stop the musket balls.
        I am digging very deeply—how clever!
        I can hide from the cannon balls.

I have my English canon:
        Theirs not to reason why
        Theirs but to do and die
        Into the valley of death
        Rode the six hundred.

        Not a valley exactly.
        Not a canon either. Not even 600.
        Colonel Despard jumped the gun
        and launched the artillery too early:
        White sparks of pain against a steel-dark sky.

Not a valley—an earth fortress, a pa
at Ohaeawai—an inner ring of hard puriri trunks,
and underground shelters, an outer palisade
of sticks and flax spruced up for the new fight,
elevated platforms inside to view the enemy,
and a ditch that passed in parts under the palisades
for communications. The pa was 90 by 50 yards in all. Reminds me

of a visit to Boston's Bunker Hill, but the American defenses
were more exposed. Despard sent his men charging
before the 32 pounder had dented the pa walls. They only
had one ladder to scale them. We had a Maori cannon—
how clever. Kawiti designed the bottom of the pa walls
to be raised and with flanking angles so the people could fire
on the troops from behind and through loopholes below the knee.
110 of the 250 British soldiers were killed or wounded
in that bright pyre, gunfire taking their feet from under them,
while ten of the hundred Maori died.

Then Kawiti's fighters withdrew in the night before
the 32 pounder finished the job. 'Friendly' Ngapuhi
chased them vainly to spare Colonel Despard's ego.
The troops stormed the pa defended by the corpses of a woman
and nine men. Ohaeawai was claimed in the papers as a win.
The troops captured a woman, sacks of kumara and potatoes.
Despard said the pa must have been designed by a European.

O the wild charge they made!
Honour the [sic] hundred[s].

Note

I am indebted to Chapter 10 "Groans of a Vain War" in Paul Moon's book *Hone Heke: Ngapuhi Warrior* (Auckland: David Ling, 2001), a brief reference in Michael King's *The Penguin History of New Zealand*, and James Graham's essay "The Battle for Ohaeawai Pa" online at <http://www.historyorb.com/nz/ohaeawai.shtml>

4 William Colenso, On the Eve of the Treaty's 50th Jubilee...

I am writing to record the activities of that little British band
who strove to do their best for the nation. My notes
are condensed because I was working for the missionary press
and the government, but I did take time to get this checked
by Mr Busby. Mr Sullivan has translated this hopefully

reliably into verse for a gift of tobacco. Lt. Governor Hobson
came off the "Herald" to begin discussions with chiefs gathered
at Waitangi. In the bay were numerous canoes—each canoe
was lead by kaituki-singers on thwarts keeping time
with their voices and inspiring their crews with gestures.

These canoes came from all directions. The Natives squatted
in front of our spacious tent where England's banner
billowed above the tasteful flag adornments.
The whites chatted A l'Anglais—the new ones were
especially happy with the delightfully situated occasion.

The customary New Zealand grey was doffed and the weather
became exhilarated with the cheerful sounds of cicadae.
While these distractions caused much sociability
among the gathered and strolling groups, the Lt. Governor,
the Reverend Henry Williams and Mr Busby were busy translating

the Treaty. Then the French Roman Catholic Bishop Pompallier
arrived in purple canonicals. Pompallier brushed past me
into Mr Busby's house where the Treaty was being translated.
He seated himself to the left of the Governor. Rev. H. Williams
immediately sat to the right of the governor, and we Anglicans

supported the cloth by standing directly behind the Reverend.
We would never follow Rome. The Lt. Governor explained
the situation to the assembled chiefs. The chiefs spent much
time arguing—many were worried about land, about freedom,
Te Kemara even stood right before the Governor with his hands

crossed in front of him as if they were shackled.
This caused convulsions of laughter. Many chiefs
implored the Governor to sit, to stay and be a father
for them. Although the Governor set down the 7th
to be the next appointed time, it was decided to meet

on the 6th. There were fewer chiefs gathered that day
owing to a disturbance caused by the distribution
of tobacco the night before. There still would have been
between 300-400 chiefs. Before the signing by the first chief,
and after a promise by the Governor to protect all faiths,

I told the Governor I did not think the natives understood
what they were signing. I felt it was my duty as their missionary
to make it clear as to the document's intentions.
The natives had told me they trusted their missionaries
and would follow our lead. The Governor thanked me

and I felt my duty discharged as Hoani Heke
          came forward to sign first.

Note

I am indebted, for vocabulary and some phrasing, to W. Colenso's *The Authentic and Genuine History of the Signing of the Treaty at Waitangi, New Zealand, February 5 and 6, 1840* (1890, Capper reprint 1971, online at http://www.enzb.auckland.ac.nz/)

5 Hanoverian London

I recently read a Marxist history of the city by George Rudé
to help me understand why so many English decided to leave

for New Zealand, among other places. I can see why now, and
with compassion. The historian says there aren't many histories

of faces in the crowd. He talked about mistreatment of
minority believers, gin's evils, class differences, diseases—

all before the Victorians' great reforms when our people were
taken into the British family of nations to be kept as children.

It's an old story of course retold by many such as Lemony Snicket
in his recently completed *A Series of Unfortunate Events*.

6 After Reading W.S. Merwin's *The Carrier of Ladders* and then Finding the *Extinct Birds of NZ* website

TAHI.

The first that comes to mind is the Huia,
which Sir Walter Buller said sang like a soft-flute.
The female had a long curved beak,
and the male a short one. A male and female
approached Sir Walter when he whistled,
and as they hopped slowly away his companion
shot them. Their feathers were prized
by chiefs, and long beaks too, for adornments.
Europeans admired the black tail-feathers
tipped with white. The Duke of York was given
a Huia feather when he visited New Zealand in 1902
and inaugurated a European fashion-craze
that most directly led to their extinction.

RUA.

The Moa is held up against Maori
for killing a food resource. We often hear
about moa and Maori in the same breath.
I agree this bird shows our humanity.
Dinornis Robustus stood two metres
at the shoulder, with another metre
to the end of the neck. You've probably
heard that museum assemblies, where
the bird cranes to its full three metres,
are fanciful—that its head was connected
most likely to an S-bend. The small ones
were bigger than a turkey. Many moa
could look a tall person in the eye.

The last ones vanished hundreds of years
ago into Maori stomachs. We're also
critiqued for the disappearances
of the giant eagle, and many other
song birds. Moe mai, moe mai, moe mai rā.

TORU.

The Giant Eagle's wingspan was three metres—
its main food was moa. It was the world's
largest eagle—the youngest set of bones
found so far is five hundred years old.

WHA.

The Stephens Island Wren was spread throughout
the North and South Island. Its common cousin
is the Rifleman. The only non-Maori
to see one alive was the lighthouse keeper,
David Lyall, of Stephens Island in
1894. His cat fetched seventeen
similar corpses not long after and so
the bird was declared discovered *and* extinct
at the London ornithologists' club
meeting held in 1895.

Moe mai moe mai moe mai ra = Rest, rest, rest there.

7 Buller's Honour

According to his entry in the *New Zealand Encyclopedia* of 1966,
Sir Walter walked around with a dark cloud of corrupt land court

practices connected with his "protracted" mediation services
in the Manawatu purchase of 1865-66. It also says that his book

on New Zealand birds made him pre-eminent in his field.
Even I've heard of Buller's birds. Again, though,

there's a smudge (aha!) on his record—the charge that he traded
bird skins for his collection, contributing to their extinction.

He spent time in London and helped to organize the New Zealand
bit of the Vienna Exhibition. He also "qualified for the Bar

at the Inner Temple", hence his Land Court work. He had a home
on The Terrace with Corinthian columns, and a wild-life estate.

He retired to London where he died in 1906 with a wealth
of letters: C.M.G., F.R.S., K.C.M.G., and honorary degrees.

8 Letters to Lord Ranfurly

Thankfully the Turnbull Library has digitized some of its collection. I had the immense pleasure of reading the letters between Lord Ranfurly and HRH The Duke of Cornwall (later King George V) about his 1901 visit with HRH The Duchess of Cornwall.

His Lordship courteously raised an unseemly incident by a group of Volunteers in Wellington protesting at conditions in their camp before their Royal Highnesses. He assured the Duke there would be an inquiry. He also noted the general and sincere

affection throughout the Colony toward the Royal couple. Lord Ranfurly felt it would have been better for them to depart from the Bluff rather than Cook Strait for Australia as the passage would have been smoother. His Lordship would be requesting

an Imperial inquiry as to the safety of the Bluff Port as it could affect the Colony's trade. Once again, in his draft letter, he assured the couple of the Colony's loyalty. Indeed, the Duke, in his six pages, remarked on the strength of the fighting men

who paraded before him. He felt secure that the Empire could draw on such strength of numbers should the need arise, as it had recently in South Africa. He also remarked, toward the end, at his pleasure on meeting Maori chiefs and representatives.

I then had the pleasure of reading Lord Ranfurly's letters from the British Museum (Natural History) for his gifts amounting to 170 native birds and skeletons: "Partly in skin, and partly preserved in formaline and including many valuable birds".

These included cormorants, and the last pair of Auckland Island Mergansers, shot by his Lordship on January 2, 1902. They were a subspecies of duck, according to nzbirds.com. The Trustees instructed Director Laukester to send their special thanks.

9 Born Again

I hesitate to point this out as I don't want to put
a propagandistic good-feel gloss on the birds
sitting in our museum cabinets around the globe,

but we have been recovering: the kiwi
boasts electrified fences up north, the takahe
thought extinct for decades now lives

next to the lighthouse at Tiritiri Matangi Island
in Auckland's gulf harbour, and numbers
of bellbirds are zooming up: it's not all bad eh.

The kakapo—our giant flightless parrot—
keeps going just, our Chatham Island robins keep bobbing,
thanks to conservationists everywhere.

10 A Decade a Maze

This little arcade of poems is like the Dole Pineapple Maze—
the hedges are thin enough to see through, and there's a
    visitor's center
where you can buy soft toys and candy. A friend took us
to see the birthing stones on the other side of the highway.
They're sacred. Many high chiefs were born there.
The stones are shaped for the human form—
they're smooth with chants. I'm a visitor here
and can see the humanity in this place. I can't see
the people who put the stones here but I can feel them.
I don't know of similar places back home.
I know of the place at the back of Uncle Jack's
where all the placentas are buried. I have heard
of our burial cave and the stones there.
But these stones are out in the open—just off
the highway, so accessible it makes me worry
they aren't safe. They look strong though—
too heavy to lift into a museum unannounced,
way too big to break.

11 Reconciling

The channel's a deep one between islands,
and inland deeper than we can throw. When
the channel broadens out to blue water
we follow shell maps of the skies

and chant. But for now we hug the coast,
concern ourselves with offshore breezes
that might push us far away from home—
we just want to catch enough to eat,

to return in time to cook the meal.
We observe the customs, say our names
out loud believing in their sound. Our
belief system is still connected

to the tide here. Allusions are ours:
light changes our way, shifts like the shore,
eases skins over frames, makes us animals
of the ocean. We've sheared into blue,

fly with the current, spray the dying light
with the spit of our shouting in fear—
we're holding on instead of letting go
as we throw our voices out. We take

rest before dawn, kneel on thwarts before
the red flickering tabernacle and pray.

12 About Anna Seward's *Elegy on Captain Cook*, 1780

She was an admirèd member of the Lichfield literati and one guesses
endeared by many. Her elegy for Honora is moving. Seward's poem
on Cook's death is enjoyable for its musical zest despite one's sensitive
leanings. Naturally, as I am consignèd to serve this Dantean subject —
my hair tied to Cook's mast, let us begin by addressing p.8 of A.S.'s
text, "And now Antarctic Zealand's drear domain/ Frowns
                                        and o'erhangs th'inhospitable . . ."
though later in the poem she does mention the hospitality and tresses
of native women. Maori are very unfairly imagined as 'uncultured'
'youths'. You know well, before they signed their names with feathers,
                            some of our chiefs' requests
Mr Governor be our father. We mistook it. I like Seward's sun ode best.

13 What If...

New Zealand was part of French Polynesia? More
Maori would drive Citroëns and Peugeots I imagine

and be more familiar with the Pompidou Centre
than the Victoria and Albert. We'd go to the lycée

and express our disquietement at the nuclear tests
under White Island, but then wave at the *Charles*

de Gaulle as it docked in Napoleon, our capitol.
Our cuisine would really be cuisine!

and like Tahiti we would be an indigenous majority
even though we'd be firmly in the republic.

I only see advantages: literary connections:
Glissant! Cesaire! and French Polynesian writing:

Rai a Mai! Henri Hiro! Renzo Piano would have designed us
a cultural center like the one in Noumea. Aue! Mais non!

2. Poetics

14 Negative Capabilities

Keats wrote to his brother about the value of uncertainties
using as an example Coleridge who would not include "a fine

isolated verisimilitude" if he could not completely account
for it rationally. Well here's to mysteries! Bill Manhire

in *Mutes and Earthquakes* talks about writing what you know
and what you don't know too. This is by way of explaining

my research methodology which is serendipitous to say the least.
I might know the name of the author, or the book, or the event,

but seldom the sharpness of the sun from the west,
the feelings rushing to my fingers as I sign my name

and my country away, Keats' desire for the madness to kiss.
This teetering on the crater has its pitfalls: the invisible crises

of critics, loose rocks, beautiful empty seaviews. There are
no paths where I'm heading. The rocks and stones landed there—

the plants were seeds blown in. My feet stumble on the newness.
Sometimes it's a city, or a symbol, I'm walking in and on.

Often I'm walking in on myself—my ancestors providing
the wide-shot—me dollying for the mid-shot and the closeup—

the moviemaker's waltz, wide-mid-close, which I really don't know
about either. I caught the idea last night from *Charlie Rose* on PBS.

It's quite good. I like Charlie, but since they've had guest hosts
like Salman Rushdie the show is more significant.

15 Review

When I was a lot younger I was reviewed by someone
who said that I should stop paying homage to other writers—

you know what? I listened to that reviewer so for a long time
I wouldn't pay my respects—I'd pretend I was writing in a vacuum,

that there was no history of reading inside me, that everything
was original breath unaffected by the airs and graces of my elders.

But here I am more than a decade later remembering . . .
It was only a stray thought. The reviewer meant well.

But sorry I've just seen a seagull tracking the up-draughts—
carried up down and sideways with a tilted glide breathtakingly

musical. Here comes another—wind enough he doesn't need
to flap about just soar, accelerate, soar so that for a moment

he thinks he's a piece of paper he's so wrapped up in the wind.
Yes this bird and that bird today are my favourite poets.

16 The Winding Stair

I had rented a little car to Boyle
where my grandfather's birth was registered,
was returning when I saw Yeats' Tower,
turned off the country highway with its sheep
reminding me of New Zealand—went in
to the cottage shop, paid the price, and sat
through the presentation. Then up I climbed
wagging my tail as I went. The stone steps
were narrow, windows were slits in darkness,
each chamber was a stanza of the great
man's dreams. The sedge and slate were repaired
for visitors like me. I recommend
one takes a drive to Coole Park too as I
missed out—fear the rental company might
charge late fees prevented that. The visit
astonished me: a cosmic accident
to stand atop the tower and gaze out
as Yeats once did, and to imagine stars
placed there, to feel his intellectual fire.
Nine years after I climb and climb the stair.

17 Seven Voices

[The First] I draw on another poet
for this structure, but then everything
is handed down—every single word,
every sign—before taps and plumbing,
before buckets and wells. A time of gourds.
[The Second] So you borrow from Senator Yeats
whose great-grandparents' meetings with Burke
and Goldsmith got you thinking about whakapapa.
[The Third] Granted they weren't your greats,
but your own great-great-greats and great-great-great-greats
you were thinking of.
[The Fourth] And the northern ones at that.
[The Fifth] From the Bay. Not the Hokianga side.
[The Sixth] So you're weaving a particular strand,
the grandest, connected to imperial and chiefly power.
[The Seventh] Not that you believe in imperialism,
nor in the power to discipline and punish.
[The First] So in humble regret I say
before the woven mat of all my genealogy
I am proud of every strand.
[The Second] That is a better way.
[The Third] Yes lay out the whole mat.
[The Fourth] Yes one curled by the toes
of dreamers and chiefs.
[The Fifth] Yes a mat pressed by many family members.
[The Sixth] That's something to be proud of.
[The Seventh] Yes, be proud of the entire family,
all our plaits—long coloured ones,
bent, stained, split, stringy, and dirty ones,
fly the whole mat like it's your flag.

18 Took: A Preface to "The Magpies"

Before we knew what our cousin signed
    for blankets, and grog, we were told in a hui
to move off the land. We wanted to argue
    and korero with our arero and puke like the tui

that flew away. The sharp beaked magpies turned up,
    pecking and squawking, frazzled and screwy.
We tried to unpick the stitches from the new no.8 wires
    and korero'd with our arero and clucked like the tui

that flew away. But no good. Our family were not understood.
    Not understood, the farmers said, shooing
us down the dusty trail. Your talk sounds like the magpies—
    all quardling oodling ardling wardling and doodling.

Do you mean korero, uri, arero, wairua, ruruhau perhaps sir?

Notes

An early draft of these prefatory stanzas for Denis Glover's "The
Magpies" was written for an essay in *Landfall* 211. In that essay, and now
also, I apologize for taking liberties with his classic poem.

Arero = Tongue
Korero = Talk
Ruruhau = Shelter
Uri = Descendants
Wairua = Spirit

19 Gesturing at the Sky

My Soul: I haven't leapt at heaven yet
so cling to this frame like a leaf.

My Self: I have been told to be suspicious
of anyone who talks of souls.

My Soul: But were they Maori? Don't they know
the feelings of people who traveled thousands of years
to have their culture turned into a game of shells?

My Self: I see the point but believe it can
be sharpened. See over there where the light
flashes red against the horizon? That's
Helen's Needle.

My Soul: Now you make fun of me.

My Self: No. It's named Sky City Casino
but Helen's people feed it thread.

My Soul: But surely the church would make a stand
against such a pharaonic creature?

My Self: Sky City paid the church for its new roof
and provides clients for its services, and before you ask,
many celebrities promote its work.

My Soul: O Mordor! Rob Muldoon couldn't have thought
this big. No wonder my family is losing money there.

My Self: Yes, but for their privacy, we won't name them.

My Soul: So the point is sharper now. How will we unseat such a thing?

My Self: This monster?

20 Redemption Song

I ended a poem in this book with a reference
to our Ngā Puhi champion, Hone Heke, who led
the first effective resistance to the British.

But I'm not a warrior. Those days were long ago.

If you wanted a war-song to belt look for a fighter
with a long spike, a musket, and a suit of armour.
You might offer him a horse, a beautiful
chieftainness to dance for him, and
a bundle of Treaty cash.

I don't even have
a Sancho Panza.

I only wield *amores*.

21 Investigator

It's like searching for Jimmy Hoffer, soil flying
everywhere, craters and police cordons, lightbulbs
flashing, traffic, loudhailers, private eyes,

surreptitious exchanges of packages,
a word dropped here and there out of the corner
of a mouth, a word cuddled up to a cigar,

eyebrows, lots of eyebrow action, and snarling,
sometimes a pet dog's or a cat's,
and talk about values, cheap ones and big ones,

then subpoenas, Congress, published proceedings,
a poem.

22 Letting the Sun Go Down

When I was a lot younger I was on a panel
at an Auckland poetry festival saying
if the sun goes up in a poem then it must come down.

What a babe! There's a lot of pressure to be clever
when you're a poet at any age.

On autopilot searching for material I scroll the news sites
I'm always reading the science and space sections
so I know about the asteroid the Japanese probe landed on
plus the rings and moons of Saturn,
and visited Google Mars

I've read about Voyager 2 hitting the end of the solar system
breaking the solar wind bubble into the enchanted evening.

Hallelujah! Hallelujah! King of kings! Queen of queens!
Forever! Forever! Praise her!

23 Elegy for Traveling

I could quote a dozen travelers on their backs
in the small hut with the little fire and the polite
note to treat the place like home. Their packs
are heavy, the rowing arduous, the flight
in a small plane rocked from wing to wing,
the pony refused to move a hoof forward despite
the whip, the sleigh stopped running
as the grass poked out of the snow, and so on,
until the travelers ended up on foot swinging
the door of the Holyford Valley hut open
let's say, in Central Otago. You've seen the imagery.
In this hut is a table supplied with paper,
and a pot of rabbit stew that warms up
in time for meals. The pens are always lying there.
All a traveler has to do is draw water
from the stream, breathe, shake the salt and pepper.
As the days pass the stew turns to roasts and taller
feasts, until the cameras have their fill
and the travelers beam videos to a tower
that relays onto an all-orbiting mill.

3. Tikanga / Customs

24 Posture Dance

Here in Hawai'i there are many performing Polynesian emsembles.
The Maori one describes the haka as an assertive posture dance.

One of my favourite pop songs is called "Safety Dance"
which also reminds me of the idea of cultural safety

first espoused by Irihapeti Ramsden so bravely in the 1980s.
Haka is for women too. To tell you the truth, it's the Maori women

who have been the most successful in advancing our culture. They
remind us "we can dance if we want to" but we're not leaving

our cares behind when we do it. The posture comes through
the very earth, from our feet grounded in the stance

of Tū. Apirana Taylor's amazing poetry comes from there,
thighs flexed in the haka stance like Tūmatauenga who withstood

the onslaught of Tāwhirimatea, lord of winds, after his parents
were separated and bleeding. So I flex my thighs and scrape

my fists on the earth. Ee ya ha ha! Let the winds blow on us,
tear at us, cause the hearts in our chests to rise. We stand.

25 Vārua Tupu
for Albert

The equivalent Maori phrase to the Tahitian
is wairua tupu, spirit of growth. Beautiful
beautiful Mā'ohi people, tangata whenua.

I see their images in a journal, a photo of Henri Hiro
who calls on the tangata to write! Write in English!
Write in French! Write in Tahitian! Which
reminds me of Ngũgĩ wa Thiong'o's challenge
to change the world and of Ken Saro-Wiwa's
Ogoni star dancing in the blackness of heaven
and of Haunani-Kay Trask's sharkskin rhythms
calling out Pele in her people and Albert Wendt's
spiraling caul of liquid fire.

We connect ourselves with poems of struggle,
hearts hammering like Martin Espada's father,
fear embraced and set free by Joy Harjo. I serve
Cervantes. He sat down on his backstep
near 60, one-armed, two whole teeth in his head,
and began to write *Don Quixote* said W.S.Merwin
as he began a reading here. Allen Curnow
recited to me "I the poet William Yeats"
and Robert Kroetsch read with the heart
of a young man, while Margaret Atwood's eros
poems rested their wings with me. Write out the lives,
write them alive, write till the fire strikes,
another fire, a torch, a whakaaraara warning cry
kia hiwa rā! kia hiwa rā! kia hiwa rā ki tēnei tuku!
kia hiwa rā ki tēnā tuku![1] Watch every terrace
of the fortress, there's an enemy climbing up,
a blaze from heaven, kia hiwa rā! my friend.

So I light a fire here in this stanza,
my small room with large windows,
carried from the fires on the hills

and the haka fires in the poets
from the processions of mysteries
and lamped freeways, from history sourced
in gin of the Fleet Ditch and Gordon Riots,
and James Cook's golden narratives
to our own kōrero neherā, our oral
bodies caressed tuku iho tuku iho down
to present hands cupped to mouths
as we plunge and rise in the ancestor ocean
shield our eyes from bullet-train rays
and think of our father Maui
who planted himself and his brothers
in the East who caught Tamanui the Sun
after the night at the crater
of the creator our mother the Earth.

Poet Henri Hiro in brotherly spirit I embrace you.
Je t'embrasse. Ka awhi au i a koe e te tuakana.
Moe mai moe mai moe mai rā e te tama manawawera,
te tama ngākau mārie hoki. He waiata aroha,
he mihi mīharo nā te kitenga o ō waiata, ō whakaaro
painga mō ngā tāngata moutere. Ka haka!
I turn back to the flame of life. Ka oriori au: tīhei mauri ora![2]

Notes and Translations

Vārua Tupu is the name of the French-Polynesian special issue of the
American literary journal *Mānoa* in which the late Henri Hiro's work,
and other indigenous Mā'ohi writing, can be found.

1. Be alert! Be alert! Be alert at this terrace! Be alert at that terrace!
2. I embrace you. I hug you older brother. Rest here, sleep here
   hot-hearted son, son of peace. A song of love,
   an astonished greeting at the sight of your songs,
   your blessed thoughts for island peoples. I haka!
   I turn back to the flame of life. I chant the breath of life!

I. LAERTES' SHROUD

I've been weaving this for years,
trying to make a cloak fit for a chief in state,
warding off the newcomers until
our sovereignty returns.

II. BOW

The proverb says never to bow your head
unless it's to a mighty range of mountains.
Another proverb says that a man will die for two
things: Women and land. Parts of me have already
died for these but I am ready to pass
my fingers through a needle to reach them.

III. SEA

The cyclops have written their critiques,
some so harsh it's hard to cross the sea
feeling easy, assured of a welcome home.
The portents for a return are wrong.

IV. ITHACA

Hawaiki ends the longing, where the soul
rests after its dive to the beloved.
We enter the great house baring our feet
and those of us who believe put on wings.

27 Arohanui

Big love, that's what it means.
Aroha Nunui means huge love.
Aroha Nunui Rawa means very huge love.
Aroha Nunui Rawa Ake means bigger very huge love.
Aroha Nunui Rawa Ake Tonu
     means bigger enduring very huge love.
Aroha Nunui Rawa Ake Tonu Atu
     means biggest enduring hugest love,
which are some of the lengths and times of our longing

The battalion changed my grandfather's
life. There's a photo from Italy with
the Duomo in Firenze not too far
behind him. I've been there too, been over-
whelmed by the Uffizi's Botticelli stanza—
overtaken I roamed the corridors
and stanzas till I returned to Venus
who I still adore selfishly. Not even

the story of course. David's copy out
in the plaza cooling his heels in poop,
the Florentine hawkers, long queues for hours
I've conflated with *A Room With a View*—
was a Merchant Ivory anyhow—
Helena Bonham-Carter, Venusian,
blushed as Maggie Smith chaperoned,
kept up polite conversazione

at the table. My grandfather was there
but I know very little apart from histories.
The mobile canteen, te rau aroha,
was paid by the Maori tamariki
of New Zealand. It kept the men going—
from desert to olive groves. Not telling
this to tell about the war though. I like
Italy. Florence was lit up at night

as I wandered the renaissance streets, thought
all was poetic: *Inferno Dante*,
inferno! I heard a man, sitting tall
on a bike outside Casa Di Dante—

I wasn't fooled, just stalling, I was chill
near where he and Beatrice his fiancee
were married. In mosaicked Ravenna
I went to her love's flame—then Venice.

Tamariki= children

29 Starboard

The starboard side rolled up as we struggled to gain our paddles—
no use clinging to the waka as large enough to hold
us. Paddles might be good flotation but it was a crazy thought.

Some of us dog-paddled to a nearby island. I breast-stroked
and back stroked, but I wasn't making any headway. I kicked
for the waka. I could see the taniwha carved into the starboard,

its paua eyes shone mercilessly into my frightened ones.
What an adventure. I'd only climbed aboard to get in touch
with my roots—it was a harmless invitation. I didn't stop to ask

the guys about lifejackets, radios, flares. It was a worthy cause.
The water was cold even though it was late summer. My teeth
were knocking. We were in the middle of the Hauraki Gulf,

millions of tons in freight floating toward the city, but not
a pound nearby. Not much to think about now but rescue. How?

taniwha=mythic guardian creature
paua=abalone whose multi-hued shells are used for adornments

30 Wake

I hide myself in a waka,
and at night raise the underworld sail where the sun and
    moon sleep,
look down the black ink inlet
    and follow the spume of Hamilton jets
eroding riverbanks holding up the land.

With coins on my eyes like cucumber-slices it's soothing
    to sail here—
the boat knows the way there—
I can feel the moon glow, the path the sun took
not far ahead—everything is coppertoned.
    I ask the sun: "Tamanui—we still own the land, ne?"
But the sun remembers Maui who hit him so hard
he still crawls across the sky. He doesn't answer.
    I ask the moon,
"Mahinarangi—we still own the land, ne?"
    The moon sighs patiently
    and points to Rona, swearing
and clinging to a cabbage tree. Mahinarangi says,
"Like her, most of you cling to the wrong things. A few
own land." I guess the distance in miles
    to my meeting with the gods
who will sift and weigh me.

31 Cape Return
for Alistair Te Ariki Campbell

Carried out by tears, songs and speeches
they make offerings on their journeys—
the atua are strange, 'plant gods, tree gods,'
who'd strike them—until the familiar
path shudders down—a heavy wave

on the shining sands of the longest beach.
Spirits flying from east and west, ridging
the spine between, meet at the headland
above Tohe's beach. At Maringi Noa
they look back, tears thundering down to join

new ones coming north. At Waingunguru
the stream mourns them. They climb another hill,
reach another stream—then a waterfall
silenced by their crossing. They continue
the last ascent, a ridge, which lifts up the cape

to Hiriki, then a sharp fall where water
lies waiting to hold them. They are expected
to drink and swallow the night, with
a chance, even then, to stay—the sentinel
there has the power to turn them back.

They continue. Desires splutter like spit
on flames. They're leaving for long Hawaiki,
to sail, dip and chant like birds forever.
The mist swarms over the last cliff, climbs off
the last piece of coast over the ocean, home.

Note

I am indebted to the "Te Reinga" entry in Margaret Orbell's *The Illustrated Encyclopedia of Maori Myth and Legend* (Canterbury U P, 1995). The entry describes the geography of the spirits' final journey.

32 A Poem for Whangarei on the Opening of the New City Library

Ngā mihi manahau mō te tuwheratanga o te whare pukapuka hou.

We touch our earth mother with tears. They connect us
like stitches, tuituia, to the sky. We are bound like them,
by our lives together, stand like these pou whakairo

raising the summits of home. Ahi kā to light them.
The world of light our tribal shelter, our whare wānanga,
our house lined by mountains and our descent.

Yet this library's genealogy touches Alexandria's papyri
as well as our whakapapa whose eyes are paua on our carvings—
who look unblinking on generations of storytellers, feeding

the talk of chiefs, memories stored and eaten like the crops here.
Our recollections take us everywhere, like the waka bringing
kumara from Hawaiki Nui, Hawaiki Roa, Hawaiki Pamamao—

to Rangiātea—how our tupuna brought food from the mouth
of Rongomai Tane to our pillar Manaia looking down on us. Praise
those who retell the praise. The people here know this land,

her rivers and mountains. Many know: Reipae and Reitu,
the sentinel rock across the harbour, the gathering whales,
tohunga talk of whales' breastbones—all meanings

of Whangarei. This library keeps the light alive, beyond
a single vein. Ahi kā is her unseen fire, the call of the ao marama
and knowledge. The Hoteo and Waiarohia are more than names—

more life blood than rivers. Our library weaves and spreads
our stories and praise forever. To hold Whangarei
close to our children, parents, grandparents—yes, for us all . . .

Nga mihi . . . = Joyful greetings on the opening of the new library.
Pou whakairo = ancestrally and mythologically figurative carved posts
whare wananga = highest school of knowledge

tuituia = to stitch or weave
ao marama = world of light
whakapapa = genealogy
tohunga = priestly experts
ahi kā = home fire
Hawaiki = ancestral Polynesian homeland
Rangiatea = Rai`atea, in the Tahitian group, regarded by many Maori as our traditional homeland
Rongomai Tane = deity responsible for bringing the kumara or sweet potato to New Zealand
Manaia = mountain at the headland of Whangarei harbour
Reipae and Reitu=deities associated with Whangarei

33 Messenger

On *Te Karere* it's like watching the best television news
from the 1960s and 70s. There's feeling—sadness, delight,
importance—and it's written into the newsreaders' Maori scripts.
We're told about the funerals around the country, and
the celebrations: Mrs Weterina Harris had a special screening
of her films when she turned 100. Her secret to longevity?
asked the reporter. Aroha, she said. Sir Howard Morrison received
his honorary doctorate from Waikato University—
his nephew Temuera Morrison (he's the Bounty Hunter
in *Star Wars: Episodes 1 to 3*) praised his work around
the world, as Sir Howard had been praising Mrs Harris' earlier.
The news show is one of the ways I'm staying in touch—
I can watch the pictures, and follow most of the Maori, with love.

34 God and Fathers

I.

Henri Hiro found god outside of church and on the lips
of the ancestors: Tangaroa is God, he said, imagine,
that God is Tangaroa—the implications.

He's a whale, he's the mind of every ocean creature
flocking like thoughts, flying between
the spaces of our god's laughing belly,
every ocean wave a liturgy that began

in time for the starlight of four billion years
to touch the salted windows of the sea.

II.

Tangaroa's priests are many-finned and eyed.
Their cassocks come in a thousand hues
as they glide the reef pews, mouth the sounds
of the lord that gives them water, and provides
volcanic votives, distributes sonar-charts of fishing nets
and other dangerous spaces of his brother
Tane whose children roam the ocean
looking for meat.

III.

The mother and father gods remind us we are children,
every single one of us: every air bubbling child.
So let's play with all our fins and toes!

IV.

So you have come to be a father for us
from the far side of our father-ocean.

V.

Since you have been our father
I cannot say you were a very involved
parent. You didn't care for us—
you cared for someone else,
Her Majesty's reputation
as a humanitarian. You didn't accord us
the respect that a parent or a governor should.

VI.

You said you would govern us, and we said
come and be our father to look after us,
those of us who supported your coming.
We thought you cared—that you were going
to share your parental skills
with us. So we bowed our heads and our words
were soon shackled in print
that said you were our sovereign,
not our father, that we were subjects
not children.

VII.

But we are children!
We play different games, and we sing
different songs. We climb different mountains
and we swim different lakes and shores.
We love to paddle waka, and carve and weave.
We love our seafood and our landfood.
We love to perform together.
We love our ancestors like your bible says
you love yours.
But how were we to know it was all words
for you, just another contract you signed

to get us before France, to avoid fighting us?
Ha! Maui would have liked to meet you.
Well done, Mr Governor, well done.
We took you to be our father. Well done.

Tangaroa = major Polynesian ocean deity

4. Personal

35 Biographical Data

A distant shore, another slip of land fished out by the trickster,
or unmouthed by Pele near the house of the rising sun,

Hale-a-ka-la on the eponymous island of Maui. Why am I so far?
Where is home now that my earth mother is Papahanaumoku?

Tangaroa himself is diasporic Kanaloa.
I am a Polynesian migrant become no longer tangata whenua here

in this State where Cook's parts lie. Hawaiki here is Kahiki,
which is at least the same as Rangiātea, temple centre of the world.

My waka has lost its k, become a wa'a, but not its mojo.
Why am I here? Am I an exile? My country has been settled

by another race, become another place: New Zealand. Yet can I say
it's better here? The climate's wonderful. When I go to Aotearoa

the chill hurts my bones and that's the warm spots! Yet I'm Maori.
I am Irish. I am Scottish. My English ancestor Wynyard ended up

governing the colony. My Ngāti Manu ancestor Pomare's name
comes from Tahiti, and I take satisfaction in that too. My selves

clap and sing dirges, shanties, and waiata to bone flutes,
bagpipes, and ribboned tambourines. My selves collect in me

and I label each with post-its. But labels don't stick to the ocean.
They don't plant themselves happily on waka prows and sterns.

I am here and I am not here. I am in several places at once.
This poem is peeling. I need some sunscreen—30+ and waterproof.

36 Hui

So you've decided to return to the Hokianga
where my grandmother came from—sold the house in
       Auckland.
Now you're waiting for a meeting of the village
to confirm your return. Your voice on the phone
tells me this is the right thing to do—to live
at your late mother's side, although there are worries.
Dad has been ill for years and needs medical care.
You have lived in the city since the 1960s,
but no, that's my worry I didn't think to tell you.
There is a family library left tucked into a meeting house—
well, you'll need to move the house to the neighbouring block
because the block it's on is owned by a distant cousin.
The details don't matter. You're going back
to a strange village uncertain of a welcome.
I've been there of course. Looked at my grandmother's grave
and recognized some of the names around her.
Such a contrast to Karetu where grandad's family
is buried. I can remember a tangi at this other village
ankle-deep in mud, slippery boards across a creek,
the pallbearers claiming the coffin got suddenly heavy
as they tried to take it up the hill to the grave.
You said your mother wanted to be buried in Karetu
so she'd be close to her children. Now you're going to her.
I don't know the place very well. I hope you'll be alright there,
both you and dad. It's such a brave thing to do.

37 Songs

We watch PBS Hawai'i a lot (it's the best channel by far).
Once there was a travel show that featured New Zealand—
this British backpacker who went to popular and local
spots. What amazed me is that he zeroed in on Maori culture.
He went to a powhiri in the far north where the welcomers
sang him *Māku rā pea*. His song in return was *Yesterday*.
He was impressed by the obvious struggle to revive the culture
in contrast to the public performances by kapa haka groups
for the tourist market. Good on him. I hope there are more
tourists like him—with a bit of candour.

38 On Flowering Ground

I. LIBRARY BEES

A house of bees holds our family story: they swarm
and hive around papers and photos, feather cloaks
and spears, carvings and weavings. They're the living
ancestors, weave dust into sweet gold, guard our story
with their lives. Our mother has turned this part
of her life to them, will raise up the meeting house
and relocate the house on our family trust's farm
so that we can all gather there and know this library
of our ancestors. The bees will follow. I know they're
going to, like an arrow, a direction—they're a part
of us too, our insect kaitiaki, dust angels—there
to remind us of ourselves in our family.

II. I COMB MY HAIR

into the hive and feel the heat of a million
wings, pollinators, tiny feelers, shed
scales, dropped in the mix till they're cleansed
by sweetly golden insect intelligence,
breaths beaten and hammered by black feet,
striped abdominals, into syrup for mother and babies,
pressing and stroking the comb, humming.

III. THIS HIVE

holds our family papers—alive with the rites of bees
who dance to the left, circle, shake stings,
rattle wings, who jig as solar guides
watching for grass and small tree shadows, to trees
flowering with the golden mean—red and yellow
pohutukawa. It's a tribal welter of sucks, slurps, slips,
bzzz, waiata, pockets spilling yellow crumbs
of half a million children darting

from a forest to a small house with a queen,
with our family library in a flowering field.

IV. IT HAS BEEN SAID

that our bodies are meadows for bees,
famous all over insectdom for our nectar
us manuka poets — they sell the fruit
of the humming in New York at organic
markets where the hum of the entire
world can be heard under the earth
and at the top of the tallest shafts —
manuka poems, pohutukawa poems
near the four leaf clover ones.

It's the smoky taste of manuka nectar
that makes the gold mean something;
it's a native secret — the finest wood
to fire our earth ovens with
the flavour. In NZ you can buy
manuka flavored bacon
so I'm sure it's in New York too,
but that isn't the right cure.

The honey has the cure, does wonders
for inflammation, and brings out
the boiling medicinal Maori in me.

39 Lunch with Frank O'Hara

What do I say? I've never read him but people have said
we're alike! How embarrassing! Ahum, I like your lunch
poems Mr O'Hara, I'd say. I can't even begin to describe him.
Oh that's good—how kind of you. Which ones? He'd ask.
Oh, you know, the ones about lunch. I order my hot chocolate.
You're a poet? I haven't been keeping up with New Zealand
poetry I'm afraid since before I was off the planet, he'd sigh.
Did you know, I'd say, there's something on the Internet
that says we're similar? He wouldn't pause for breath.
Isn't that funny! People think the strangest things.
I'll Google it. It was very nice to meet you, he'd say.

40 Rangatahi

I'm no longer a member of the rangatahi—
I'm getting long in the tooth, it's been decades
since I read *The New Net Goes Fishing*,
a fantastic book, one of New Zealand's best.

The rangatahi generation are out there
hip-hopping and rapping in the reo.
They don't know how lucky they are.
I remember Fred Dagg's other song

which was my favourite in Onehunga Primary:
"If it weren't for your gumboots where would you be?"

rangatahi = new net, i.e. new generation

41 Waiata Whaiaipo: Lover's Song

I tune the heart-string
                         bring it to the key
that sings of love's wings
                         Huia feathers
        gliding from the hair
                         of my beloved

42 Love

Twenty years ago I wrote out of a desire
to love. And now that I know love—
everything she wears—I keep writing. I'm the same.
Only the love has changed. You know this.
I don't know you but you have met this love
in love. The photographs, the dinners, prove
your love's so personal, she flames differently,
but you have met this love. Sometimes lovers reach out
like lines form couplets, doubling and spilling vowels
in their spiraling. They climb stairs in hand,
place their head in their lover's hands, drape leis
over each other, drink, play the scent's forceful rites
that buds chests and groins, flowering to touch desire.
I want you to know all this love.

43 Boyle

My first home was with my mother who lived solo
in the 1960s until I was six months old. My grandmother
came to visit and told dad off. From then on
he supported us. I'm very lucky to know my family
at all. Mum said that her former employer,
who managed a bakery, would have adopted me.
He was of Yugoslav descent. So I could have possibly
grown up believing I was from somewhere else
completely. As it was, mum was brave.
In 1967 there was no domestic purposes benefit.
I don't remember, of course, the small flat
she must have rented on her own. My earliest
memory of a home was in Boyle Crescent
which was near the place the hippies and poets met.
We lived there till 1974, well past the summer of love
but still a love child. Funnily enough,
dad's father's birth certificate was registered
in Boyle, Ireland. I have no memory at all
of my grandfather who died in his eighties
when I was only one. My father's had bad health
recently, but he was always good value
to be around and he still is. He did amazingly well
like his whole generation after the war.

44 Ata Wai

The water shifts into a slower rhythm
as it gathers under the deeper section
below the bridge. The bridge was originally
two railway sleepers, but after twenty years
one of them finally rusted through
and it was dragged off beside the water pump
on the bank. The other one never did rust,
we still use it, though my grandfather
doesn't live in the house anymore.
He's in the urupa on the other side,
just up the road from the marae.

The deepest and slowest part of the rhythm
is the water hole past my great-grandparents'
house which is still in the family. It's great
for jumping into. They're also
in the family urupa on the opposite hill from
their place. I'd like to know about a lot
of things that happened there, but then
not everything's for knowing.
All I know is that they're still there,
that my uncles and aunties are looking after
the village, and to call it home.

ata wai = slow water, term used in Maori translation of 23rd psalm
urupa = cemetery

45 Rumination

Why is it that cars quack? with a remote
flutter of fingers cars sing like birds, gobble
like turkeys, whistle like panpipes,
want to fly? But the feathers are metal,
the wings are rubber, some with chrome spinners,
some taller than SUV's that roar
like dinosaur ancestors of birds.

I want to fly too. But staring into a river
finds fins on catfish that rub by each other,
catfish with leptospirosis worrying
about the dwindling shallows
chock a block with old carparts
and McDonalds wrappers, cigarette stubs
that sent smoke up into skyward feathers
and the litmotes of bird throats.

My throat is raspy and smokey,
washed by sinus streams, glasses
of chlorine, and the odd flu. We're
all rivers of course, between banks
that wind their way to the Styx,
looking for the easiest way there.
So cars cross bridges. My poems flash
their headlights and beep.
Watch out for the cops!

There's a speedbump! A rut!
Honk! Gobble. Quack.
Fly up to the Tantalus or the Pali highway
oh rubber wheels, oh T-Rex tracks
of the majority. In Hawai'i we have
an interstate freeway—brainchild
of Eisenhower who saw
Hitler's autobahns. What a lineage!

Where's the happy balance?
But the heart valves flutter—open
and release their streams, provide
the pressure for everything: Like the metal
furnaced in thousands of degrees,
that rusts in streams by the thousand.
So bellow cars! Make your doors flap!

46 Spines of Smoke

My family is a forest torn out of the ground—
life goes on.

We lift our shaggy afros and the birds nests topple—
blue-cupped babies cheep.

We're a slow diaspora—linger in the region,
hope our Maori leaves will be our calling cards,

give us chances to plant. Yet leaves have veins,
have sap that we grieve every winter.

There is no winter here and none of our soil.

47 Vissi D'Arte, Vissi D'Amore

I've seen *Tosca* once in Auckland, but it wasn't Kiri Te Kanawa—
I have her 04 recording with George Solti—she's amazing.
I've seen her command Mozart's *Don Giovanni*. I like arias

very much—they're so Maori. Her recording of Maori songs
is too stiff, however. Funny that. I'm so proud
of Dame Kiri. She used to work in the telephone exchange
with my Great Aunt who says she met her again much later

backstage at Covent Garden. Touched by a star.
Yet in *Vissi D'Arte* there is anguish. It comes from somewhere
in her—I can only guess. Where does the music come from?
There's the coordination of players, the sweating loving

conductor, the care as for a baby, as for a mother,
the keening and the holding of notes, the entreaties
to our better selves. Ah Puccini! O fragile Madam Butterfly!
O mio babbino caro! Superbo! Bravo! Homai o pakipaki! Clap!

Note

Since writing this poem I have seen Mr Bean's 2007 movie set partly in
Paris, where the main protagonist loses his wallet and is forced to lip-synch
music in a marketplace so he might earn bus fare to Cannes. Movingly in
the picture he moves through a musical range, from break-dance to yes *O
Mio Babbino Caro* by Puccini, the latter number being the most successful
in winning a crowd and money for the trip. As Pound said, "Only emotion
endures!"

48 My Uncool Popular Tunes

Not an interlude music wheeling the air
as a harpist snatches air with each stroke
a xylophone comforts time
                    a harp reels out the soloist
Kiri's singing Puccini again
                    follows the song with the notes
grieves as she breathes
                    Bravo! Superbo! Bravo! Bella.

The playlist jumps to "How to Dismantle an Atomic Bomb"
and "Vertigo" swinging to the music—it's mad
the riffing! I like playing air guitar over keyboards
yeah
        yeah
                yeah
                        yeah
                                yeah
                yeah yeah yeah
                yeah
                        yeah
                                yeah yeah!

The next on my top 25 is *Vissi D'Arte again*—
I Googled it for a translation, which I'm condensing (apologies to
        Puccini):
I lived for art and for my love, I gave jewels for the Madonna's
        mantle,
                I sent songs to the stars and heaven.

                The next song is "I say a little prayer" sung by Aretha.

Before I tell you the next one I have to say that poems
are a far more affordable form of ITunes—I'm on an email list
where I get a new poem everyday, for free!

"Blowing in the wind" is next.
Then Kiri's version of "Un bel dì vedremo" from *Madama Butterfly*,
I like the last tragic moments. My favourite singer of my teen years
was Barbara Streisand. Here she's singing "Some enchanted evening".
It reminds me of dad's shower singing, "There will be such wonderful
    things to do . . ."

Another teen hit, for me, was Andrew Lloyd Webber's musicals.
Here Sarah Brightman sings "Tell me on a Sunday please" from *Song
and Dance*. I guess I'm leaving in silence, but I'm not running off
in the pouring rain, not calling as they call my train . . .

But that's no note too end on. Hallelujah! Hallelujah! Hallelujah!
Hallelujah! Hallelujah! For the Lord God omnipotent reigneth. Reign
    for ever,
for ever and ever, for ever more.

Here's Barry: There's many times we've shared love and made love.
It's just not enough. My darling I can't get enough of your love, babe.

49 Kick-started by a Bananarama Track

Last night I was dreaming I was locked in a prison cell.

Well, perhaps if I was writing this, I wouldn't say "dreaming".
I'd probably say "screaming" but who am I to argue this?

Bananarama have sold millions of records and now they've
sold me "Love in the First Degree" on ITunes! You can't argue

with the bottom line. How many times must a man look up
before he can see the sky? Well, if I was writing that

I'd say "person" not "man". But you can't argue with Bob Dylan!
It's like the eye of the needle from earlier in the sequence,

but you can't argue with God. It would only mean heartbreak
for me, as Aretha sings. For me there is no-one but you.

I could quote you something from Nirvana but the guitarist
and the drummer are a bit loud. The song is called "In Bloom".

Too much of anything is not good for you baby, as Barry White
says. He makes the counter-argument that he can't get enough

of your love. I scream your name, he says. I don't know why,
don't know why, he sings. How can I explain what he feels?

50 Civilization

In the computer game *Civilization* it's possible to build
an empire—develop muskets, and rockets, and nuclear weapons
over a week of playing. I've done it. I know it's a real possibility.
Other civilizations compete with your one. There are maps
you can download too. I downloaded one of Australia
and New Zealand. The Polynesians haven't got a civilization
in the game. There are a few barbarians at the beginning
which the civs beat up for their maps and their gold.

Of course I'd rather we weren't represented. That way
I can maintain the fantasy. My son used to play it too.

51 Note to PJ

Mark Twain said that you go to heaven for the climate
and to hell for the company—which reflects
merely on the weather of the north and south
poles of Polynesia, respectively, I think.

We borrowed *The Lion, the Witch and the Wardrobe*,
directed by New Zealander Andrew Adamson, on Netflix.
We recognized some of the snowy scenery. What struck me

were the heroic roles Patrick Kake and Shane Rangi played
as centaurs. After Peter Jackson, whose films I like,
it was a personal relief to be on the good team
as I'm tired of seeing Maori depicted in the pits.

It's good for our kids to see that.

52 When I Meet People Here

I can't help serving up the lamb chops. I tell them
I'm from a country with forty million sheep and four million people—
it always crops up. I don't tell them about the bank ad

with sheep roaming through Lambton Quay, or the poem by Cilla
McQueen where everyone is surrounded in cotton wool and the whole
country is a suburb although I think I'd feel better telling them these
things

because it makes me feel homely, like I'm wearing the softest lamb's
wool sweater. I wouldn't tell them I can't bear the feeling of wool
against my skin, nor about a boyhood of scratchy scout jerseys and
prickly tramping

socks. I tell them Auckland is bigger although architecture in Honolulu
is much better—I like the buildings here for the muted style, clean
lines, that surfaces are concrete, not glass. The tower here is called
'Aloha'.

Auckland has too much colour—buildings shove and yell like the
traffic. Yet a beach at home really drips with pohutukawa blossoms
like a telecom ad. A mountain at home (on TV) is sprinkled with snow.
Here

they're sprinkled with NASA telescopes. The army at home for me is
Arch Hill barracks up the road from our house which is the part-time
reserves' base. Here the army comes with ICBMS in the hills, the
airforce

with stealth bombers and satellites, and the navy with the Pacific
nuclear submarine fleet and visits from the USS Nimitz. That reminds
me to visit Pearl Harbor—although we're slightly worried about a
terrorist

attack there. Still,our family goes to Mass here, and I still believe this is Polynesia. The names of the Hawaiians' ancestors are everywhere: palaces, beaches, mountains, streets and parks. Just look at the signs.

Then I ask them where they're from.

53 Northland Museums

I. THE BISHOP

This, the Bishop, being the most northern Polynesian museum
is the first in the line stretching south to Aotearoa

and the Tai Tokerau. This Northland Museum
is named for one of the inheritors of Kamehameha himself—

Princess Bernice Pauahi Bishop. It has its beauty and its echoes—
the hall of the ali'i with the flower staffs denoting royalty

and oh how they are present, they are so present
it makes you wonder about the past they are so present.

What moved me most were the broken eyes of the whakairo
from a pataka in the Polynesian Hall. Broken eyes all through

the Maori carvings—why don't they repair them? I mihi
my ancestors, their proud hardwood mana, their assertiveness

even with cut eyes. In the gift shop I buy a postcard,
touch a monograph by Te Rangihiroa, am gratified

that I have earned the kama'aina rate for my Bishop ticket.
On the way out the shop keeper remarks on my greenstone.

It seems too easy, too little protocol, my mere residency
granting me status to enjoy the wealth of ali'i. It's a question.

II. Annex

On the way out of the main museum buildings it's hard to avoid
our Easter Island ancestor, unfinished or decapitated, another
 question

as I slope toward the planetarium. They have a video
of the International Space Station next to a small exhibit

of the paths the ancient waka took to settle the Pacific.
It's a strange take, to compare the ancients with the latest

technology, a combination of the world's wealthiest
and/or most scientific nations. It would be fairer to compare

the waka with the reed boats of the Celts, or the square rigs
of the Romans, but you see waka were superior. More is unfair.

I cannot fathom the annexation.

III. The British Museum

In the atrium of the Auckland war memorial museum,
cluttered with multiple donation takers, I let myself
through—look up at the marble figure above the revolving door
and remember my time in London, the Parthenon marbles,
sounds of Turkish Explosives, the audiovisual recreation
of the British. A grand welling leaps up my throat.
How, how can they take all these things? So many things
they can't display them. The only woven Maori sail
in the world is tucked away there. The helpful guide says
it was in a Maori exhibition a few years ago . . .

What to do about this? Accept? Forgive? Adopt the levitating
lotus and smile? So I smile and notice. I smile and watch
them go about their business on our land. I smile and watch
them derive value from ancestral objects. I smile and smile.
But it's passive aggressive. I smile when I'm aggrieved.
I smile when I stroll past the Celtic cases with their fine-wrought
gold amulets. Past Assyrians and their stones. Onwards
I march, inspecting the imperium from within this museum.
Smiling. I'm contemplating the temperature controls,
and the elaborate security for the theft. I smile knowing
they're well protected. That they'll go on forever.
Will we go on forever? Will we be the range of mountains,
standing by night and day, in all weathers hugging
our culture and our language? How can we be as strong
as the walls and pillars of the conquerors' museum,
stronger than marbles scattering dust, stronger than history?
Our strength is still a miracle to me.

IV. THE BOTTICELLI STANZA

Entranced, enchanted, delirious, Italiano, heady, sensational,
airy, beautiful, supine, oh staring starry wondrous
woo and swooning, beauties renaissance beauties

framed and gold by my heart so golden and a scallop
and a suit of armour amour again the sally
this is the Uffizi where a Leonardo and a Michelangelo

and a Dante all breathed nearby and caught the heart's sails
on canvas and sailed the wind tossed seas
shook the breeze of petals landing like timpany

such a sweet crush the perfume filled the Botticelli room
and wafted as far as Auckland past Hotunui

of my childhood and its red cellophane ceiling lamp

magic triple magic so magic I summon Dante's ghost
like the tongue in cheek cyclist, outside his house,
calling 'Inferno Dante, inferno!' And I descend, ascend there.

v. Omapere

We stayed at an artist's cottage
just below the south Hokianga headland
of Araiteuru, not far from the pillar of our Ngapuhi
house, Whiria. These places have some of the oldest names
in the country derived directly from Hawaiki
and our ancestor Kupe. We went up to the headland
on our last day there, the turnoff just past
the gas station, and adventurously for us
we followed the track on foot through the scrub
until we reached the rocky point.

The view was amazing even on a calm
sunny day. There was white mist coming off
the beach which arced out beyond the pyramid shaped
dunes beneath which a village lies. I knew this
from a visit to the information centre there
which was also the local museum. It had glass cases
full of intricate shells, photos of settlers,
genealogies and other records. There was hardly
anything about the local Maori, except
for the reference to the village.

Yet as I said, Omapere is near the main pillar
of our tribal nation. I didn't know that the first time—

ten years ago now—I was scouring Northland museums
for our stories. The volunteers were very friendly though.
I've learnt since then we keep our stories somewhere else.

5. Foreshore and Seabed Poems

54 For Sure

It bothers me I can't be closer. Sent to the furthest region of Polynesia,
top of the triangle. Where to next? Rapanui? But I can't speak Espagnol!

If only I could lie down with my country again, feel her rocking tides—
rejection! Where's the love?! So much hope! We pulled together

a flowering tree of Maori, a massive pohutukawa bursting
with the brightest spray, birds singing their hearts out. What happened?

Our tree was too brown. Its roots were cracking the barracks wall
and the Maori were breaking the safe. There were too many of us.

Only room for a few or it would spoil the hors d'oeuvres. We might've
planted 'Maori spinach'. Smoke from the hangis would cloud their eyes

and noses. Yet I love my country. I do. I desire her more than ever.
I know her body as a lover. My sighs are locked with hers.

55 After the UN Rapporteur Supported Maori Customary Rights

If it was tattooed in Maori there'd be an indigenous Universe
in this curvy groove—but it's a problem of bleeding translation,
to spit the worldview from a disembodied tongue, no shy body,
no swaying—a paintbrush tongue over eyes, face, hupe-nose
and wide toes, broad brow (is that me you're picturing, eh?), but
Maori prose—that first named the land—is almost wahangū, muted.
The verbs, nouns, adjectives, tenses, all the key teeth thrown
on the table are English played with by ancestors of Westminster

& Trickster, nibbed by Councillors & Scrabblers, ammo for Radical
& Stately mouths, chuckled at in cartoons of Ewen Me. English
boxed on for 13 *centuries* since Caedmon like fish and chips love?
cuppa tea love? where's my CliffsNotes on *The Odyssey*, darling?
English broadcast from the moon, is spoken by our family, plus
it's orbiting Saturn! Yet Maori liberty is still recognized by Earth.

Hupe = mucous
Wahangū = mute, quiet

56 Ngā Tohu Whenua

My tipuna put the third signature on The Treaty. He drew
a spiral. Many of the marks we are told are X's. I think a spiral
is the appropriate image. Not for the coiled energy flow, as
in a frond, or the whakairo delineations expressing the rank
of a person, spirals and patterns conveying the thoughts and spirit
of the carver—bound to his people's ethos—but for the descent
a spiral can emit, not blood, but the spiral that leads to the pit:
into a holding cell, or a pit housing the tangata whenua.
We have gone from pito, our birthright under Tane-nui-a-rangi,
placentas punching out kauri and totara, to this, a pit.

X is inappropriate. X reduces one to a line on the page, a mark
collated and paraded to justify muskets with stiff bayonets,
speeches denouncing traitors and savagery, while brown ribs
jut and ribs inside marae decay and fall away. At the Turnbull
giftshop I bought a poster of my ancestor's pa of Otuihu
being bombed by H.M.S. North Star's twenty-six guns. The account
is in the microfilmed journals of the enemy. Our ancestors
cannot tell their story themselves. You read so far

and the meaning will leave you. How did one continue, faced
with death? Civilized savagely, ancestor eyes of extinguished
lives, their photos in acid-free folders, display cases,
catalogued and tagged. But where are they remembered?
On every point in the country, forever.

57 Suite of Poems Addressed to Prime Minister Helen Clark

I'm disappointed in you for not protecting us mainstream
Maori. We had due process rights that needed to be explored
like Europeans explored us. We might not have been
property owners, it's a complex issue, but the courts
were willing to help us come to an understanding.

You removed the courts, Helen. You took away one
of the reasonable and peaceful tools we had for redress.
So this is personal. You have nearly three and a half million
New Zealanders in one Treaty basket filled with snappers, oysters,
green-lipped mussels, jon dory, caviar, plus 90% of the land

which they inherited, bought, mortgaged, rented out to each other
and some Maori, and 700,000 New Zealanders in your finely woven
kete probably given to you by some beautiful weavers who trusted
you to look after the mother they struggled for, and cuddled for a
thousand years.

That group of New Zealanders has kinas and pipis, rock oysters,
piopios picked out with safety pins, and mussels they dived for,
plus the fish they caught in their Treaty boats, and there's still
space in their kete. A lot of their land is leased out for pepper thanks
to generations of Ministers of Maori Affairs, and most of their land

is carved into blocks even though it's called Maori. Many of them
want to jump into the full basket, and many are happy
where they are thank you. I know not all Pakehas are wealthy,
but I know a lot more per capita are compared to us — read
your Key Statistics reports, especially the Maori Health ones,

ask your responsible Minister to do something off the air,
ask why you're going to lose more Maori. Helen, why didn't
you leave Justice alone? She didn't vote against you. No one
likes their sunny day, the chance to make spirals
in the sand, swept away . . .

ii. My Treaty Quota

I didn't think I was going to write a sermon but thinking
about the price of shellfish at Foodtown inspired this. It's far
easier for a snapper to pass through the eye of a needle
than for wealthy people to get to heaven. So how will
they get in, eh? How are all the people who support
the confiscations going to wind their way through?
I'm not sure who's going to be waiting at the paua-shell gates
to check ID's and make sure they had all the right injections.
I like the ancient Egyptian system—the country's great artists
will adorn Her needle with special effects—Helen's Column,
Her Name and the Treaty laser-lit in hieroglyphic images
of a wearable-art dress, and a hole will be poked atop the needle
to align with heaven. But as a Maori voter
I'd get a sea-urchin (a kina) to plug it with.

iii. My apologies to the Egyptian people

for inaccuracies regarding the needle.
I admire your fantastic culture. Your pyramids look
like Aoraki mountain white and gold with snow.
In the Metropolitan Museum there was a fleet of boats

for the journey to the House of Ra. My son did a school project
on Osiris, lord of the Underworld, and we saw the travels
of river souls. He used our photos from the Met in his essay.
At the Honolulu Art Academy there are papyrus scrolls
where you can print your name in hieroglyphs on an inkjet.
I wonder what symbols would make up Helen Clark's —
a kina on a needle? To be a leader requires a certain bluffness,
an unnatural certainty about oysters, an inhuman

quality to prevent the peasants rising up
to question your inhumanity. So I accept that
your job is difficult. My job in writing this
is a difficult one too. Once I read you a poem, Helen,

about how I wished I could drop the politics
and write in freefall. But there's so much gravity here.

IV. Okay okay

Okay, okay, I'm overdoing the histrionics. You aren't that bad
personally. You don't remember me but I remember you —
it was an honour to meet you! You were our Prime Minister!
You were very nice! Even at my little poem reading
the media were there to ask you questions about something.
On the news that night there you were answering the questions
while I was the shoulder to the right of the screen.
I love your arts policy. I still have friends in your party.
It's great that you went on stage during the wearable art awards.
And thank god for democracy. I love it! The ideals, the freedom.
Sure it can get Churchillian — it's imperfect as Sir Winston said.
This poem is part of the freedom of expression in our country
and here in Hawaii, I respect your right to disagree, as President
Bush often says to ignore people's points of view. I know
you've met him and more often and for longer than I met you.

The other time we met was when I saw you get out of your
car at Auckland airport. I know you have a very tough job,
but my job is tough too. It's my job to remind you
and the governments that follow what you have done
to many Maori people and what you should be doing too.
So I'm going to serve out my complete term. No one
elected me. Only my heart, my nose, my liver, my stomach,
my veins and all the blood they carry, all the cells, each hair,
my whole body is gathering to use its two Mixed Member
Proportional votes for Love and Happiness to change this.

58 Poetics Tunnel

Aue! I've gone wandering down the political winds
without testing the vehicle in a tunnel first—where
are the political poetic precedents I hear the critics hum?

True. They're thin on the ground nowadays.
I could cite some—Juvenal, Ovid, Virgil, Aristophanes, Olds, Plath,

Shakespeare, Swift, Blake, Baraka, Cesaire, the Irish bards
after the English invaded. I guess New Zealanders
don't tend to write overtly

politically. What a shame for our literature in English.
Of course if you can read Maori you know already
that's the predominant mode, the haka being the most

political and the most popularly known form that we have
for New Zealand English or Maori speakers. The haka
is a form where you put your whole physical being
and perform it until you are completely exhausted.

But this is just a test.

59 One Art

The Queen of Heaven is a needle
whose eye is a spiral drilled with the same metal
that printed the facsimiles of our polite sounding Treaty.

Through this spiral passes all who signed
the unsaid in the other ones' tongue.
The reverend translators, ritual forecasters,

recorders of weather and statistics of stones
building stories of a New Zealand that has risen far higher
than the battlements of Windsor, but only literally.

Tens of thousands of men, women, children,
were struck dead by the diseases of the Queen of Heaven,
by visitors whose history had warned them of this.

Yet the only way forward
is forgiveness, and we ask them to forgive us
for our wrongs as we forgive them.

60 Fancy That

I'd just remembered Temuera Morrison's amazing role in
    Star Wars.
They cloned him—millions of Maori marching through the galaxy
for the Republic, and then the Empire. Back here on Earth
we have the real thing and it takes much longer to build our
    numbers.
We're getting there. *Statistics New Zealand* is watching us:
the Prime Minister and the Party know we're increasing.

61 Canst Thou Draw Out Leviathan with an Hook?

A D-shaped shackle failed, felling an earth wire
strung between Otara and Otahuhu,
that caused Auckland's blackout one Monday, a string
plucked by Maui, the city a gasping fish
spun around until all its contents—gamblers,
addicts, families—stumbled out from dead lights
into sun. They stole looks at their reflections

in the dimness, while the rest of the country
following *One News* noticed how important
some Aucklanders noticed the city to be:
Asian and Australian cities would now
have shinier scales and swim further because
of this cut. Important people asked big questions
about the wire that holds the city, but they have

forgotten a tradition. Sometimes Maui
gives it a tug for fun, spends a few idle
hours tickling the big fish of its Wellington
myths: King Kong, the Polynesians from Mordor,
the canonical costumes and makeup. Who
can blame him for his jealousy? These people turn
billions of dollars over. Maui just has

a fishing line, and the customary
reeling of credits

62 Let's Karanga The Whole Thing Off

You say potato and I say kumara
You say Gidday and I say Tēnā koe
Potato, kumara, Gidday, Tēnā koe,
Let's call the whole thing off.

You say Treaty and I say Tiriti,
You say justice and I say hegemony,
Treaty, Tiriti, justice, hegemony,
Let's call the whole thing off.

I say kia ora and you say begorrah
I say iwi and you say kiwi,
Kia ora, begorrah, iwi, kiwi,
Let's call the whole thing off.

I haka "ka mate" and you say "Go AB's"
I say "Wannabe" and you say "yeah a Steiny",
Ka mate, go AB's, wannabe, Steiny,
Let's call the whole thing off.

If you say oysters? and I say yes,
and give back the foreshore and seabed,
Then we'd better call the calling off off
Let's call the whole thing off.

Ka mate is the first line of the All Blacks haka.
AB's stands for All Blacks rugby team
iwi = tribe
Kumara = sweet potato

63 Manawawera

Burning air—Haka—Fire air
for the hot heart (manawawera)—
Oh I could say things!
                    But not in English.
I'm made a moa by critics,
tarred, feathered and stuffed.
But I'm a mainstream Maori, that's
the water from the river to the seabed.
So I dive often into the cool wai Maori, our reo.

wai Maori = fresh water
reo = language
moa = extinct bird, once the tallest in the world

64 Someone Asks Us Why

Why did you begin by speaking in Maori?
I didn't expect the question from another Maori writer.
The other writers on the panel didn't either.
We were at *The Going West Book Festival*,
talking about Maori drama. I couldn't quickly
say why. But now I have an answer—
I did it for the mana of our reo,
and our way of life. There weren't many
people there who could understand me,
but they could feel the spirit.

Our language is too beautiful to die.

65 It Will Leave You

The path wells out
of the valves slipping air
with a shove from throat to chords,
past the uvula striking
tongue muscle, and a tooth,
another tooth to curve the air
through upper and lower lips,
sparks stroked from grey mass:
a word, a glorious word.

66 The Sneeze

Comes out of your soul
below your upper jaw
woosh beyond muscles
or a big breath on the note
of 'C'—wheee!
It's your spirit singing
out the friction
of nose-hairs, each mote
a wind generator,
a gush to brush
the throat—
a wave of air.

67 Greenstone Monologues

I. Te Wai Pounamu

The dark green water is full of white eels
that slide into hook shapes, spirals, push bones
out like clubs or rounded needles
but the water is stone.

II. A Spiral

Sound is a spiral in a shell,
but I haven't seen greenstone trumpets
just the ones seeded in the sea.
Yet we choose this form,
the spiracular, to make our lips
puff out a poem.

III. White Eels

They're the veins.

IV. Hook

This is useful for catching fish
when it's made of bone, but I've never
seen a greenstone hook catch anything
but the hair of my beloved.

V. Clubs

Once I lifted Te Rauparaha's
which was heavy—he was a relative

of my Ngati Raukawa ancestor
who brought the people south
from Maungatautari
to the Kapiti coast.
We (Ngati Manu) are all very proud
to have this ancestor
in our whakapapa.

VI. ROUNDED NEEDLES

These are adornments that drape
the ears of my beloved, and sit
at her chest checking the pulse
of her love.

VII. STONE WATER

Not a literal truth. Metaphysics.
The sea an island rests in
so it soaks itself in greenstone.
The terms pounamu and mauri
are often connected, but it's more
than life-force, it carries
the gods like a waka does.

pounamu = greenstone
mauri = life force or essence
wai pounamu = greenstone water, name for the South Island
Ngati Manu = the subtribe in the far north of New Zealand that the
writer belongs to

68 Spiralling Ground
for Kateri, Cape Croker Reservation, Nawash First Nation

I touch your cloak of cedars here
    stroke your face and body
press feet onto your belly
    walk through swamp on beaver boards
throw sticks to spirits catching this Canada Day weekend.

Earth is still mother here still cools my feet amid wild flowers
heels pressing boardwalk into beaver territory, miles of path
               for heels to drum
and trees singing green tongued choruses licking air
licking birds licking the singing molecules of creation

we—my feet and I—are fat candles led by bears and snakes
dogs and beavers lighting paths
    through nature and we are native
        born to nativity
    surge over timber
        into and out of life
    our lives calling and singing:
           you are here we are trees and rocks
           we are beings dancing in our being

    prints on earth filling lungs with tongues of earth

we are earth people with an eye to sky
divinities' sails and oars across sky

calling names of stars to guide us home

to sounds of leaves
whose roots draw sound

round throats that orbit
green tongues recycled in the ground

Rondo. Rondo earth. Rondo.
Listen. Rhythm. Listen.

You can be a circle fence
for ceremonies. You can be a dancing light.

You can be turning wheels
as they drive us rocking and rolling
                              out of sight.

69 Karakia
for Bruce Stewart

I touch Papatuanuku my earthmother
     give hands up to Ranginui
my skyfather
     then beat both wings of the heart
skull it down through the pelvis
to a rosewater bowl
filling with stones: chance/angst/loneliness/failure
dip hands in this sprinkle
     heads in clarity pass the speech of people on
blush and touch make love slowly (be careful)
we slide in a round of writhing
weeds that thrash a jive
expressed in a loud way (I'm out of my circle)
persevere beat your heart's wings
     fly out to greet them
shout 'Hii!' (hee) to the ground
shout 'Haa!' to the sky
through these veins people give and take
     fine as those crossing a petal
     floating on a bowl
health to you brother (we hongi)
     health to you sister (we kiss)
splash your paddles
breathe deeply drink up
we've got a chant of unbroken
     tones to toast!
a meeting on respected grounds
an open sound so pure it shakes the host

karakia = prayer
hongi = Maori form of greeting by pressing noses
haa = breath

Lightning Source UK Ltd.
Milton Keynes UK
UKHW010657170121
377156UK00001B/63